WHERE PEOPLE LIVE

Living in the Mountains

Neil Morris

FRANKLIN WATTS
LONDON•SYDNEY

 An Appleseed Editions book

First published in 2004 by Franklin Watts
96 Leonard Street, London, EC2A 4XD

Franklin Watts Australia
45–51 Huntley Street, Alexandria, NSW 2015

© 2004 Appleseed Editions

Created by Appleseed Editions Ltd,
Well House, Friars Hill, Guestling, East

Designed by Helen James

ISBN 0 7496 5835 5

A CIP catalogue for this book is available from the British Library.

Photographs by Corbis (AFP, Paul Almasy, Tiziana and Gianni Baldizzone, Bettmann, Kit Houghton, Ray Juno, Wolfgang Kaehler, Layne Kennedy, Richard Klune, Charles & Josette Lenars, Gail Mooney, David Muench, Francoise de Mulder, Douglas Peebles, Caroline Penn, PICIMPACT, Chris Ranier, Roger Ressmeyer, Reuters, Galen Rowell, Royalty-Free, Jon Spaull, Vince Streano, Paul Stuart; Eye Ubiquitous, Keren Su, Brenda Tharp, Paul Thompson; Eye Ubiquitous, Vanni Archive, Pierre Vauthey/CORBIS SYGMA, K.M. Westermann, Adam Woolfitt, Alison Wright, Michael S. Yamashita), Ariadne Van Zandbergen/OSF/Earth Scenes

Printed in the USA

Contents

Introduction

Mountains have always fascinated people. Many ancient groups saw them as holy, or sacred, places. From the **foothills**, mountain peaks appeared to touch the heavens. Despite this, some people decided to make the mountains their home, learning how to cope with steep slopes, wild winds and freezing winters. They built mountain villages, and some of these have grown over the centuries into towns and even larger cities. Modern roads, railways and bridges have made them easier to reach. Many people from other areas like visiting mountain regions because they enjoy climbing up, skiing down or simply enjoying the view.

Home of the Greek gods

To the ancient Greeks, Mount Olympus was the home of their 12 most important gods. These included the king of the gods, Zeus, and his wife, Hera. Zeus was the cloud-gatherer, who could pour rain and hurl thunder down from his mountaintop home. His nine daughters, known as the Muses, also lived on the slopes of the divine mountain. Mount Olympus is the highest point in Greece, rising to a height of 2,917 metres at the eastern end of a **chain** of mountains that divides the provinces of Thessaly and Macedonia. Today many people enjoy climbing to the **summit**, and there are ski resorts on the mountain's slopes.

▲ *This village lies in the Ural Mountains, a huge **range** that runs north-south for 2,000 kilometres through Russia. It forms a natural border between the continents of Europe and Asia.*

Kurdistan

The Kurds are a **Muslim** people who live in a mountainous region, known as Kurdistan, that stretches across southern Turkey and northern Iraq, as well as parts of Syria, Iran and Armenia. Over centuries the Kurds have adapted to life in the mountains. They traditionally herd sheep and goats, and grow **crops** such as sugar beet and cotton. Though many Kurds live and work

 Stephanie Peak, at the top of Mount Olympus, is also known as the 'Throne of Zeus'.

in cities today, they have often been **persecuted** and return to the mountains with their families during times of trouble. The Kurds are said to be the world's largest **stateless** minority people, and their aim is to have their own independent nation.

 In the Bekaa Valley in Lebanon, poppy seeds are an important commodity.

5

Early Settlement

Many ancient civilizations developed near the coast or on the flat land of river basins. But some groups of people chose to explore and live in the mountains, where they felt safe from attack by any others who approached from below. Some of the earliest mountain cultures grew up in the Andes of South America, the longest mountain range in the world. Tribes of **hunter-gatherers** were roaming the slopes of the Andes by 11,000 BC or even earlier. This was a time of **climate** change, and as ice melted and the weather got warmer, some groups settled there. They farmed the land, built villages, and from about 1000 BC several different cultures developed. The Chavín

 The Quechua people of Peru still make rope bridges in the ancient Inca style.

culture, which was at its height from about 900 to 200 BC, was the most widespread early culture in the region. It was followed many centuries later by the civilization of the Incas, who built a vast empire throughout the Andes.

People of the White Mountain
Monte Alban (or 'White Mountain') lies on a mountaintop, overlooking the modern city of Oaxaca in southern Mexico. Founded around 500 BC, this was the capital of the Zapotecs, who

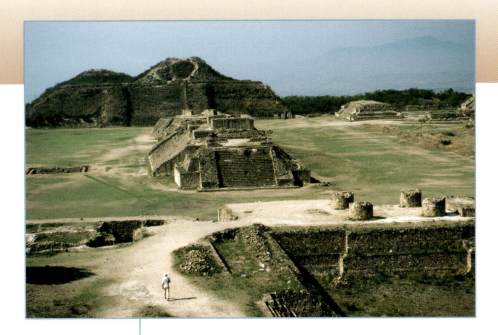

The Great Plaza at the mountaintop location of Monte Alban. The Zapotecs abandoned the city around AD 750.

over many years levelled off the top of the mountain. Then they built a ceremonial city around a rectangular Great Plaza, with palaces, temples, and tombs. During its greatest period, between AD 250 and 700, Monte Alban's population grew to about 30,000. The rulers, priests, artists and warriors who lived there were supported by **tributes** paid by other tribes in the surrounding **valleys**. The Zapotecs also mined the mountains for obsidian (a glassy, volcanic rock) and traded this with others.

Machu Picchu

The Incas built a town on a hilltop to the north-west of their capital of Cuzco. At a height of 2,350 metres, Machu Picchu was surrounded by places that were sacred to the Incas – mountain peaks, and a fast-flowing river in the valley below. The town had a plaza, temples, and a palace for visiting royalty. The buildings were made of granite and covered with steep, **thatched** roofs. This royal estate may have housed up to a thousand people, including farmers who tended terraced, or stepped, fields outside its walls.

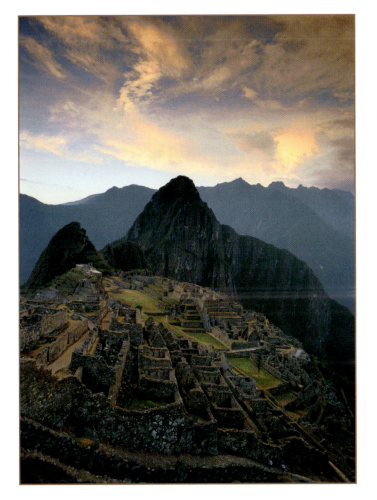

Machu Picchu was abandoned in the 16th century, and its ruins were rediscovered in 1911. Today it is a popular destination for tourists on the Inca trail.

From Village to City

People who roam the mountains have always moved with the seasons. The Native Americans who lived on the high **plateau** between the Rocky Mountains and the Cascade Range, for example, moved down to the valleys during the winter. In the summer, they went high up into the mountains to hunt, and groups such as the Nez Percé put up shelters covered with brush or matting. These were easy to take down when the group moved on. In other parts of the world, mountain people built villages with permanent homes. Over the centuries, villages grew into small towns. In modern times, some even developed into huge cities.

Alpine town

The small town of Sankt Moritz lies high in the Alps of south-eastern Switzerland. It grew on the site of a settlement built by Roman soldiers around 50 BC. They probably chose it because of its mineral **springs**, which are still famous.

▲ *This small village lies in the High Atlas mountains of Morocco. Most of the villagers are Berbers, who were probably the earliest inhabitants of the mountains and deserts of the North African coastal region.*

Sankt Moritz lies in an alpine range called the Rhaetian Alps. Its highest peak stands more than 4,000 metres.

The growing **alpine** village became a fashionable summer resort in the 17th century, and over the past 100 years has developed as an important winter-sport centre. It is the site of the world-famous Cresta Run for toboggans, and the Winter Olympics were held there in 1928 and 1948. Today, many of the 6,000 population still speak Romansh, a language that is spoken only by people in the mountains of their region.

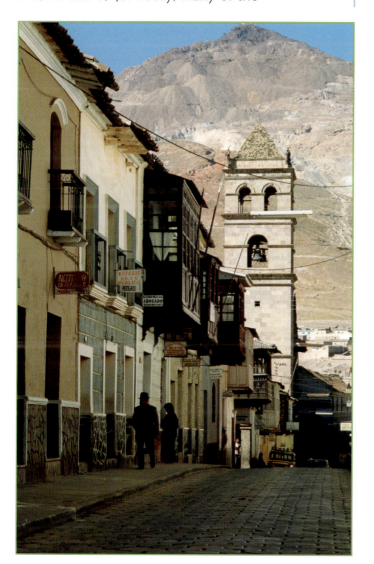

Exploding population

Potosí was founded soon after 1545, when silver was discovered in the mountainous region of southern Bolivia. According to legend, the mining settlement's name came from a Quechuan Native American word meaning 'explode', because the early settlers heard the mountains rumbling around them. By 1650, Potosí had a population of more than 150,000 and was probably the highest city in the world. When the silver had been exhausted, people mined tin, as well as copper and lead. Today, Potosí is Bolivia's leading industrial city, producing electrical goods and furniture.

*Potosí still has many beautiful buildings from the 18th century, when Bolivia was a Spanish **colony**.*

9

Farming

Living in the mountains has always given farmers two special problems. The first is the great difference between the seasons, making it difficult for humans and animals to stay high up in the mountains during the cold, wet winter. Wild mountain animals naturally move down to warmer valleys at that time, and farmers soon learned to do the same. The second problem is the difficulty of growing crops on sloping land, as soil gets washed away by heavy rains and blown away by the wind. Early farmers, such as the Incas, found the answer to this by digging out flat terraces and surrounding them with walls.

▲ *In New Zealand, sheep are allowed to **graze** high up in the mountains during the summer months.*

Moving with the seasons

Farmers move their livestock up or down the mountains according to the season. This practice is known as transhumance. It is common in all parts of the world, including the high Himalayas and the alpine regions of Europe. In the Swiss Alps, farmers bring their cattle down to lower levels in the autumn, before the first snows cover the high pastures. In the Kohistan region of northern Pakistan, whole farming families move

In Austria and Switzerland, farmers bring their cattle down to sheds for the winter. The animals wear cowbells so that they can be heard if they stray from the herd.

up the slopes of the Hindu Kush from 600 metres in the winter to higher than 4,000 metres in the summer. The families move between settlements at up to five different levels, where they grow grain and keep oxen, sheep and goats.

Terraced fields

After creating flat farming land on the mountainside, the Incas built walls at the top of each terrace, so that rainstorms did not wash

their fields away. They had to bring soil up from **fertile** valleys below, and then they dug **irrigation** channels that connected the fields to streams. Their descendants still use the same system to grow maize and other crops. In the south-east Asian countries of Indonesia and the Philippines, as well as in China and Japan, many hillside terraces are used for growing rice. Asian farmers also use clever irrigation systems, because rice grows best in very wet fields.

The use of terraces in hilly regions such as this in China lowers soil erosion.

Volcanoes

When a **volcano** erupts, it can be very destructive and dangerous to people living nearby, as well as to their homes and the local environment. Vesuvius, a famous ancient volcano in Italy, suddenly erupted in AD 79 and covered the nearby Roman town of Pompeii in a blanket of ash. Thousands of people were killed. The volcano is still **active**, yet millions of people live in the nearby region. This is true of much more mountainous areas, too. On the volcanic island of Java, in south-east Asia, large numbers of people live off terraced rice fields on the slopes of **dormant** volcanoes. People know that volcanoes bring benefits along

 *In volcanic regions such as Iceland (above) and New Zealand, **geothermal** power plants are used to produce energy for homes.*

with dangers. Volcanic rocks are put to many different uses, and sulphur deposits can be used to make chemicals.

Mount Etna

Etna is a huge mountain, rising 3,323 metres on the Italian island of Sicily. It is an active volcano, erupting regularly, and its volcanic ash makes soil on the lower slopes very fertile. This soil and the warm climate make ideal growing conditions for oranges, lemons and grapes. The Sicilians are used to living in the shadow of Etna, and they are grateful for the attention it brings to their island. Thousands of tourists visit Mount Etna every year.

Mount St. Helens

The Cascade mountain range stretches for about 1,100 kilometres near the Pacific coast of North America. Many of the range's mountains are volcanoes, and one of them suddenly erupted in 1980. Mount St. Helens had been dormant for 123 years, but suddenly it came to life with an explosion that blew the top off the mountain. Huge chunks of rock were hurled into the air, and clouds of ash billowed into the sky. Fifty-seven people and countless animals were killed, millions of trees were flattened, and buildings, roads and bridges were damaged.

▲ *The fertile slopes of Mount Etna are ideal for growing grapes and other fruits.*

◄ *The 1980 eruption took more than 300 metres off the height of Mount St. Helens.*

13

Getting Around

T ransport and communication are always more difficult in the mountains than in lowland regions. For moving goods, people have traditionally used pack animals, such as mules and horses. As people and animals zigzagged up and down mountains, they made trails for others to follow. The Incas used llamas to carry their goods, and they also built paved roads on steep hills and along the spine of the Andes Mountains. They added bridges across valleys and tunnels through mountains. Bridges and tunnels later made it possible for wheeled vehicles (which the Incas did not have) to travel much more easily in mountainous regions.

 The Laerdal Tunnel runs under the Jotunheimen mountain range in southern Norway. Opened in 2000, it connects the country's two largest cities, Oslo and Bergen. At 24.5 kilometres, it is the world's longest road tunnel.

Passes and bridges

People have always looked for the easiest and quickest ways to travel over mountains. The Romans followed several routes across the Alps when they headed north. Their main passage became a major trading route in the Middle Ages, followed by a proper road in the 18th century and a railway completed in 1867. This is the famous

This suspension bridge crosses the Royal Gorge in the Rocky Mountains of Colorado. The road bridge – at 321 metres above the Arkansas River – is the highest road bridge in the world.

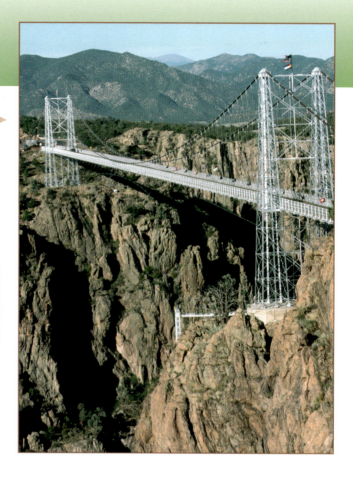

Brenner Pass, which since the 1970s has had a motorway running over it. This modern road links Austria and Italy, crossing valleys and **gorges** on high bridges called viaducts.

Mountain railways

For more than a hundred years, people have been building railways up mountainsides by using the rack-and-pinion system. This helps pull a train up the mountain by engaging the teeth of a **cogwheel** in a track between the two normal rails. A mountain railway runs up Mount Snowdon, the highest point in Wales, and one of the most famous railways climbs the Jungfrau Mountain in Switzerland. An alternative that is very popular with tourists is the **cable car**, which suspends carriages from an overhead cable.

The Jungfrau railway moves passengers 1,400 metres in about 50 minutes. The top station lies at 3,454 metres, and is reached through a 7-kilometre long tunnel.

Mining and Quarrying

Throughout history people have used mountains to mine for metals and minerals. The slopes of hills and mountains are particularly useful, because they allow miners to go deep underground by digging a horizontal tunnel. This is called strip mining. Mountains are also used for quarrying limestone, sand and gravel. In **quarries**, workers use drills or blast the material out with explosives. In opencast mines, metals such as copper are dug out of a big hole in the ground. Some of the world's largest copper mines are found in the Andes and Rocky Mountains. Villages and towns have grown near these mountain mines, but there is always the danger that they will become **ghost towns** when the mines are exhausted.

▲ *Slate from the Dinorwic Quarry in northwestern Wales is exported at Caernarvon, a seaport on the Menai Strait.*

Gold rush

Many of the world's mountain ranges are rich in metals and minerals. One precious metal has attracted people to the mountains more than any other – gold! In 1859, there was a great gold rush

Pikes Peak, in the Rockies, stands at a height of 4,301 metres. Pictured in the foreground is one of the many unusual limestone formations belonging to a public park called the 'Garden of the Gods'.

in the Colorado region of the Rocky Mountains. Wagons rolled in to the mountain range near a place called Pikes Peak, and some lucky people made a fortune. Today, during the summer months, hikers climb up a trail to the peak, while others take the cog railway. In winter, these are popular skiing slopes.

Coal and iron

The mountains, hills and valleys of Wales were once famous for their mines. South Wales had coal and iron mines. Limestone was traditionally quarried in the Cambrian Mountains, while there were many slate quarries near Snowdon in North Wales. Today, most of the mines have closed, and many of the towns and villages that grew up around them have grown much smaller.

Blaenavon, at the head of the Afon Valley on the fringe of the Brecon Beacons National Park, had its first coal mine in 1782. By the 1920s, the town had more than 12,000 inhabitants, most of whom were dependent on the coal and iron industries. Over the last 50 years, however, its mines have closed, and Blaenavon's population has halved.

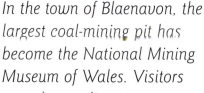

In the town of Blaenavon, the largest coal-mining pit has become the National Mining Museum of Wales. Visitors can also see limestone quarries, furnaces and old ironworkers' cottages.

The Roof of the World

 Tibetan monks wear splendid costumes to celebrate the Chinese Tibetan New Year in Beijing, China.

Tibet is a self-governing region of China. It is surrounded by tall mountains, including those of the Himalayas, which separate Tibet from India, Nepal and Bhutan. The plateau on which Tibet lies has an average height of more than 4,800 metres, and the lowest parts of its valleys are higher than the tallest mountain peaks of most countries. For this reason Tibet is known as the 'Roof of the World'. Tibetans are very religious people, following a form of Buddhism called Lamaism. Before the Chinese took over the region in 1951, one in every five Tibetan men was a monk. Their highest spiritual leader, called the Dalai Lama, was forced to flee to India in 1959.

Tibetan life

Most Tibetans live in the south of the region. There the fertile land allows them to grow their main crop, barley, as well as wheat and vegetables such as potatoes. The main Tibetan food is barley flour, and the main drink is Chinese tea mixed with salt and yak butter. On the northern grasslands, **nomads** move around with their herds of sheep, goats and yaks, on

Tibetan nomadic shepherds follow a traditional way of life. This camp lies near Mt. Kailash, in China.

the lookout for the best pastures. The nomads live in rectangular-shaped tents made of yak hair, which are easy to take down when they move on. In the coldest winter months, they move down to the southern valleys. There most people live in stone or brick homes with flat roofs.

Land of the gods

Lhasa (meaning 'the land of the gods' in Tibetan) has been the capital of Tibet for more than a thousand years. It lies at a height of 3,660 metres in the Himalayas and is home to 140,000 people. It was once known as the Forbidden City, because Europeans and other visitors were not allowed in. Today, backpackers and others visit Lhasa to catch a glimpse of the Dalai Lama's former winter home, the Potala Palace. Many tourists also come to see and climb the Himalayas, and many Tibetans – like the neighbouring Nepalese – make a living as mountain guides.

Today, the 13-storey, 117-metre high Potala Palace is a museum. It was originally built in the 17th century and contains more than 1,000 rooms. The palace overlooks Lhasa from its hilltop.

Traditional Houses

Many mountain people traditionally build their houses of wood, because the lower slopes are generally well forested. This is still the case in the European Alps, where timber chalets are popular. In the Himalayas, on the other hand, most Tibetans live in stone houses. This was the case with the Incas of the Andes, too. Many centuries ago they built solid homes in the mountains. They used blocks of granite for the walls, and covered their houses with a thatching of tough grass supported by wooden roof beams. Some Andean people live in similar houses today.

Swiss chalet

The traditional wooden houses of the European Alps, especially Switzerland, are called chalets. These were originally small shelters for shepherds, but today they are often quite large and can house more than one family. Chalets are basically designed to keep out the cold. Their long, sloping roofs hang down over the walls, so that snow doesn't fall on windows and doors. The windows are usually small, to keep the warmth in, and are covered with wooden shutters. Logs for the winter are often stored beneath the building, and a large south-facing balcony is useful for sitting out

▲ *Some nomadic Kyrgyz people still wander the highland areas of the Tien Shan Mountains, between Kyrgyzstan and China. They live in round felt tents, called yurts, and move down to the lower slopes in midwinter.*

Snow on the roof of this chalet in Switzerland actually helps insulate the interior from the cold weather.

during the warm summer months. Swiss chalets are very popular with winter skiers and summer hikers.

Highland huts

The highlands of Irian Jaya, the western half of the island of New Guinea, are home to the Dani and Yali people. They live in small villages, where they keep pigs and grow sweet potatoes. Here the climate is generally warm and wet. The women and children live in small round huts, which are thatched to keep out the rain. The men live in a larger house in the middle of the village. But in recent years, copper and other metals have been discovered in these mountains. A whole town has grown up around one of the mines, called Tembagapura, or Copper City. Industry and tourism are changing the homelands of these mountain people.

Villagers in the Baliem Valley of Indonesia work together to maintain their traditional way of life.

Avalanches and Landslides

People who live in the mountains are constantly aware of the danger of falling rocks, mud, or snow. The danger is generally much greater in winter. **Avalanches** can have many different causes, and scientists group them into three main kinds. 'Wet-snow' avalanches usually occur in late winter and spring, when melting snow makes an unstable base for snow and ice at higher levels. 'Dry-snow' avalanches are made when masses of powdery snow break loose and form huge snowballs that gather speed as they thunder downhill. In a 'slab' avalanche, a massive chunk of solid, icy snow breaks away and slips down the mountain. Landslides of rocks and earth happen in a similar way, and heavy rain can turn them into a dangerous mudflow.

Snow barriers

The very best barriers against sliding snow are trees, which help to break up an avalanche. People did not realize this years ago, when many trees were taken down for timber or to make

▲ *Climbers at Hilden Peak, in Pakistan, are witness to a dry-snow avalanche.*

wider ski slopes. In many parts of the world, trees are now being planted again above mountain towns and villages. They are helped by artificial barriers, such as high fences, which also slow down and break up the falling snow. In some

These avalanche fences have been put up above the village of Wengen, in Switzerland. The Swiss Institute for Snow and Avalanche Research conducts tests on protective barriers and gives out regular avalanche warning bulletins.

places, experts use explosives to keep snow from building up, and they advise locals and visitors when there is an avalanche warning.

City danger

Almaty lies in the foothills of the Tien Shan Mountains of central Asia. It is the largest city in Kazakhstan, with a population of more than one million. Unfortunately, this is an earthquake region, and Almaty has suffered from landslides and mudflows. To try and stop these dangers, engineers set off explosives and deliberately caused a landslide in 1966. This blocked up a gorge above the city. Seven years later the artificial dam stopped a mudflow from sliding any farther. Since then the dam has been raised even higher to protect the people of Almaty.

Almaty (or Alma-Ata) was founded as a fort by the Russians in 1854. It was virtually destroyed by earthquakes and landslides in 1887 and 1911. It was the capital of Kazakhstan from 1929 to 1997, when it was replaced by Astana.

Winter Resorts

Mountain towns and villages all over the world have grown in recent years as skiing and other winter sports have become more and more popular. The first important resorts were in the European Alps. In 1924, the French town of Chamonix staged an 'International Winter Sports Week', which later became known as the first ever Winter Olympic Games. Lying at 1,037 metres, Chamonix is the nearest town to the highest mountain in the Alps, Mont Blanc. Although it has a population of less than 10,000, Chamonix has seven cable cars, including the highest in the world. This carries passengers up to a height of 3,790 metres. Many of the local people who live in winter resorts are involved in tourism, catering for the many thousands of new visitors they get every year.

Medieval town

The alpine town of Innsbruck (meaning 'bridge on the river Inn') is the capital of the Austrian province of Tyrol. It was founded as a market town in 1180, when it belonged to a Bavarian count. It later came under the control of the Habsburg rulers of the Holy Roman Empire, before being returned to Bavaria and then Austria. It has always been important because of its position on trade routes through the Alps. In the

▲ *The small village of Lake Placid stands at the foot of the Adirondack Mountains, in the state of New York. In 1932, 306 competitors took part in the third Winter Olympics there. In 1980, Lake Placid hosted the Games again, and this time there were more than 1,000 competitors.*

mid-20th century, Innsbruck became one of the most important health and tourist centres in the Alps, with many ski resorts nearby. The Winter Olympics were held there twice, and today the town has a population of 118,000.

Banff

The town of Banff, in the Canadian province of Alberta, was named by a Scottish-born statesman and fur trader after a North Sea **port** in his

Nestled in the Alps, Innsbruck, Austria, provides ideal conditions for ski-jumping competitions.

homeland. The town grew after the Canadian Pacific Railway arrived there in 1883, and two years later the region around it became the first national park in Canada. The town lies at a height of 1,387 metres on the eastern slopes of the Rocky Mountains, and the surrounding park is famous for its wild animals, including bears, moose and deer. Further up, towards Lookout Mountain, there is a new ski area called Sunshine Village. Though it has a population of just 6,000, Banff attracts more than three million tourists every year.

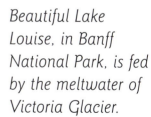

Beautiful Lake Louise, in Banff National Park, is fed by the meltwater of Victoria Glacier.

Mountaineering

People used to climb mountains only for practical reasons. They wanted to cross a range, or they were hunting or looking for animals that had strayed. Sometimes they would use their skill and knowledge to guide travellers across mountain passes. Then eventually people began to see mountain climbing as a challenge, because no one had ever been to some of the highest peaks. The sport of mountaineering was born when a doctor from Chamonix climbed the highest peak in the Alps, Mont Blanc, in 1786. A century later, French, Swiss and Italian guides were helping mountaineers climb all the high peaks of Europe. People then turned their attention to the rest of the world, and the highest peaks of the Andes and the Rockies were climbed by 1898. By the end of the 20th century,

 The Italian poet Petrarch climbed to the 1,909-metre peak of Mont Ventoux, in southern France, as early as 1335. Today, a road leads up to the radio beacon at the top.

all of the world's highest mountains had been climbed, many with the help of local guides.

On top of the world

The highest goal of all mountaineers is the highest peak. The world's highest is Mount Everest, named after a British Surveyor General. Tibetans call the Himalayan mountain *Qomolongma* (meaning 'goddess mother of the world'), and to the Nepalese it is *Sagarmatha*

Tenzing Norgay and Edmund Hillary in 1953. The Sherpa people of Nepal are skilful climbers of the world's highest peaks.

('summit of heaven'). The first expedition to Everest took place in 1921, but it was another 32 years before the peak was conquered. Two climbers reached the 8,850-metre summit on May 29, 1953: a New Zealander named Edmund Hillary and a Nepalese Sherpa named Tenzing Norgay. Tenzing had climbed on Everest several times before 1953, but he had never reached the summit. When he did, he left an offering of food at the top of the world.

Mountains of the Moon

The Ruwenzori Mountains lie on the border between the African countries of Uganda and Congo. According to the ancient geographer Ptolemy, they were once known as the 'Mountains of the Moon'. They were seen by the explorer Henry Stanley in 1889, and first climbed to their summit at 5,119 metres by the Italian mountaineer Luigi Abruzzi in 1906. Abruzzi had already climbed some of the highest mountains in Alaska and would later go on to scale Himalayan heights. Today, there is a national park at the foot of the Ruwenzori (which means 'rainmaker' in a local African language). The Amba and Konjo peoples grow beans and sweet potatoes on the lower slopes.

Despite being just north of the equator, the Ruwenzori Mountains are capped in snow. The mountains are shrouded in clouds for most days of the year.

Problems and Conservation

Modern ways of living are changing our mountain landscapes. In many parts of the world, mountain forests are being cut down to provide timber. This leaves slopes bare and can lead to increased avalanches, landslides and floods. In other places, mining has had a great effect. All over the world, tourists wear away soil and destroy vegetation as they look for mountain adventure. Hikers, climbers and skiers sometimes leave litter. All these problems can be avoided, however. It is important that we all try to look after the world's mountains so that we can go on enjoying them in the future.

▲ The Blue Mountains are a southern part of the 'Great Dividing Range' of Australia's eastern continental rim.

Noah's mountain

According to the Bible, Noah's Ark landed on Mount Ararat after the great flood. Today, the 5,185-metre high Ararat (also called Agri Dagi) lies in eastern Turkey, very close to the borders with Iran and Armenia. The mountain is sacred to Armenians, who believe they were the first people to appear in the world after the flood. An ancient Persian legend refers to Ararat as the birthplace of mankind. It also lies within the Kurdish homeland. Today, the northern slopes are in a military zone, and people are allowed to climb Ararat only on rare occasions. Modern political problems have closed off a mountain that has great meaning for many local people and visitors.

National parks

In order to look after their mountain habitats for the future, many governments around the world have set aside nature reserves and national parks. There are protected areas in the world's three biggest mountain ranges. The Rocky Mountain National Park was created in Colorado in 1915. It has more than 100 peaks at least 3,000 metres high. High in the Andes of Peru is the Pampa Galeras National Reserve. In the foothills of the Himalayas, Nepal's Royal Chitwan National Park provides a safe home for black bears and mountain goats.

There was once a village and a monastery high on Mount Ararat's slopes, but they were destroyed by an earthquake in 1840. This was just 11 years after the first successful ascent.

Daisetsuzan National Park was established on Japan's northernmost island of Hokkaido in 1934. The park's snowy slopes attract area skiers.

Glossary

active (of a volcano) May erupt at any time.

alpine Relating specifically to the European Alps mountain range, or generally to high mountains elsewhere.

avalanches Large masses of snow rapidly falling down a mountainside.

cable car Cars suspended from an overhead cable used to carry passengers up and down mountain slopes.

chain A group of mountain ranges.

climate Weather conditions over a long period.

cogwheel A toothed wheel.

colony An area that is ruled by another country.

crops Plants grown by people for food.

dormant (of a volcano) Not active, but not completely dead.

fertile Having rich soil and producing good crops.

foothills The lower slopes of a mountain or mountain range.

geothermal Produced by heat inside the earth.

ghost towns Towns that have been abandoned.

gorges Deep, narrow valleys with steep sides.

graze To eat grass and other plants.

hunter-gatherers People who hunt wild animals and gather fruit and other food.

irrigation A supply of water directed to a dry area to help grow crops.

Muslim Referring to a follower of the religion of Islam.

nomads People who wander from place to place to find food and grazing land.

persecuted Treated cruelly.

plateau A flat area of high land.

port A place where boats can dock, load, and unload.

quarries Places from which stone is cut or blasted.

range A group of mountains that lie side by side.

springs Sources of water that flow out of the ground.

stateless Not being a citizen of a country.

summit The highest point or top of a mountain, also called the peak.

thatched Made of straw or grasses.

tributes Payments in goods made as a sign of dependence.

valleys Low-lying areas of land between mountains.

volcano A mountain with an opening where molten rock and gas come from deep underground.

Index